ABRAHAM LINCOLN

THIS EDITION
Produced for DK by WonderLab Group LLC
Jennifer Emmett, Erica Green, Kate Hale, *Founders*

Editor Maya Myers; **Photography Editor** Kelley Miller; **Managing Editor** Rachel Houghton;
Designers Project Design Company; **Researcher** Michelle Harris; **Copy Editor** Lori Merritt;
Sensitivity Reader Ebonye Gussine Wilkins; **Indexer** Connie Binder;
Proofreader Susan K. Hom; **Series Reading Specialist** Dr. Jennifer Albro

First American Edition, 2025
Published in the United States by DK Publishing, a division of Penguin Random House LLC
1745 Broadway, 20th Floor, New York, NY 10019

Copyright © 2025 Dorling Kindersley Limited
24 25 26 27 10 9 8 7 6 5 4 3 2 1
001-345874-May/2025

All rights reserved.
Without limiting the rights under the copyright reserved above, no part of this publication may be reproduced, stored in or introduced into a retrieval system, or transmitted, in any form, or by any means (electronic, mechanical, photocopying, recording, or otherwise), without the prior written permission of the copyright owner.
Published in Great Britain by Dorling Kindersley Limited

A catalog record for this book is available from the Library of Congress.
HC ISBN: 978-0-5939-6629-7
PB ISBN: 978-0-5939-6628-0

DK books are available at special discounts when purchased in bulk for sales promotions, premiums, fund-raising, or educational use.
For details, contact:
DK Publishing Special Markets, 1745 Broadway, 20th Floor, New York, NY 10019
SpecialSales@dk.com

Printed and bound in China
Super Readers Lexile® levels 620L to 790L
Lexile® is the registered trademark of MetaMetrics, Inc. Copyright © 2024 MetaMetrics, Inc. All rights reserved.

The publisher would like to thank the following for their kind permission to reproduce their images:
a=above; c=center; b=below; l=left; r=right; t=top; b/g=background
Alamy Stock Photo: North Wind Picture Archives 16, Science History Images 29; **Getty Images:** Archive Photos / Fotosearch / Stringer 36, Archive Photos / Kean Collection / Staff 15, Archive Photos / Matthew Brady / Buyenlarge 34cb, Archive Photos / MPI / Stringer 4-5, Archive Photos / Museum of Science and Industry, Chicago 6, Archive Photos / PhotoQuest 25tl, Bettmann 7, 19, 30, 33cb, 40-41, 43, Bettmann / Alexander Gardener. 42t, Corbis Historical 31tl, 33cr, Heritage Art / Heritage Images 26, 37, 39, 42cr, Hulton Archive / Buyenlarge / Grabill 13, Library of Congress / Corbis / VCG 22, Popperfoto 31b, Universal History Archive / UIG 34tl, 34tr, Universal History Archive / Universal Images Group 23;
Getty Images / iStock: aristotoo 18b, visionsofmaine 34-35b; **National Army Guard:** Courtesy of U.S. Army Photo 17

Cover images: *Front:* **Bridgeman Images:** © Huntington Art Collections / © Huntington Library, Art Museum, and Botanical Gardens;
Back: **Dreamstime.com:** Dmytro Lomonovskyi cla, Staurora72 cl, Aleksey Vanin cra

www.dk.com

This book was made with Forest Stewardship Council™ certified paper – one small step in DK's commitment to a sustainable future.
Learn more at www.dk.com/uk/information/sustainability

ABRAHAM LINCOLN

Justine Fontes, Ron Fontes, and Matt Myers

Contents

- **6**   Frontier Life
- **12**   The Bigger World
- **16**   Captain Lincoln
- **20**   Building a Family
- **22**   From Congress to Countryside
- **26**   Candidate Once More

Abraham Lincoln in Richmond, Virginia, near the end of the Civil War, April 1865

30	Wartime President
36	An Unexpected Friendship
42	The Last Casualty of the War
46	Glossary
47	Index
48	Quiz

Frontier Life

Abraham Lincoln was born in 1809 in a log cabin in Kentucky. His family was poor. He never finished school. Nobody thought he would become the most respected president in the history of the United States.

A replica of the cabin where Abe was born

Young Abe grew up in the early 1800s, when Native Americans were still fighting to keep their lands. Slavery was allowed in many states. Black people could be bought and sold like animals. They had to work all their lives for no pay.

The Lincolns were white, but they didn't like seeing any people suffer. When Abe was seven, the family moved to get away from slavery. They settled in Indiana, where slavery had been made illegal.

Life in this new place was hard, and everyone had lots of chores. Abe helped his family cut down trees, so the logs could be used for a new cabin. Abe fished and hunted to help get food. He followed bees to find honey.

Abe didn't have to go to school. But when he could, he thought of learning as a special treat. He and his sister, Sarah, happily walked several miles for the chance to study with other kids.

Abe later said he went to school "by littles"— a little now and a little then.

Abe went to school in a small, windowless cabin called a "blab school." Students would "blab" their lessons out loud over and over, until they knew them by heart.

Abe's mom died when he was nine. Abe was heartbroken, and his father was too busy to offer much comfort. But the next year, another Sarah came into Abe's life.

Sarah Bush married Abe's father. She had three kids of her own. Now, the little cabin was crowded but happy. Abe's father had forbidden Abe to read when he had chores to do. But Sarah thought learning was important.

Leaders from History

After George Washington led the army during the American Revolution, he was elected the first president of the United States. He served two terms but refused to run for a third. He believed that staying in power would make him too much like a king. Benjamin Franklin was an American inventor, writer, and diplomat. He believed in the power of reason and free speech. He worried that American self-government would fail unless people governed wisely.

George Washington

Benjamin Franklin

Abe would gladly walk 50 miles to borrow a new book. He copied down ideas he liked. He wrote about subjects such as cruelty to animals and how American government worked. He read about leaders, including George Washington and Benjamin Franklin.

The Bigger World

Abe loved a good story. At church, he watched the preacher wave his arms, shout, and even whisper to keep people's attention. Outside, Abe would entertain his friends with his own performance.

In those days, lawyers and judges would travel from town to town. They set up court where it was needed. Abe loved to hear the lawyers speak. He memorized their fancy words.

But Abe's favorite speakers were funny. They entertained people with stories spoken in ordinary words. Abe decided he'd be a new kind of public speaker. He would know all the big words, but he would never show off.

Traveling Courts
In the mid-1800s, most Americans lived far from a courthouse. When they had disagreements that needed to be settled in a court of law, they had to wait for a judge and lawyers to come to them, usually on horseback or by stagecoach.

Abe worked on farms until he was old enough to ferry passengers across the Mississippi River on a flatboat. At 22, he transported goods down the river to New Orleans. Abe was fascinated by the big city, but he was upset by what he saw there: Black people in chains, being sold at a slave market.

By then, the Lincolns had moved to Illinois. Abe got a job running a store. His customers loved his stories, his kindness, and his honesty. His spare time went to reading. He wanted to learn all the things he'd missed by not going to school. He convinced a schoolteacher to teach him about history, law, and politics.

The more he learned, the more he saw ways that America could change and become better. The country seemed stuck, unable to truly become the land of the free.

The cabin Abe and his father built in Illinois in 1831

Captain Lincoln

In 1831, Lincoln tried politics. His goal was to serve in the state legislature, but war interrupted his plans. A dispute over where Native Americans could plant corn turned violent, and young Lincoln joined his local militia. The men picked Lincoln to be their captain because he was well-liked and honest. Lincoln never fired a shot, but later he joked that he gave plenty of blood for his country—to mosquitoes!

Native American refugees during the final battle of the Black Hawk War, 1832

When he got out of the army, there were only two weeks left before the election for state legislature. Lincoln didn't win—that time. But he kept trying. Over the next few years, he talked to people at dances, community projects, and even wrestling matches. He won voters over with his charm and common sense.

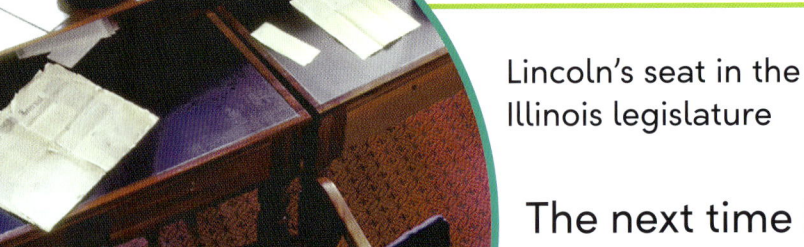

Lincoln's seat in the Illinois legislature

The next time he ran, Lincoln won. In 1834, he moved to the Illinois state capital. There, he continued to expand his mind, reading every law book he could get his hands on. He became a lawyer. He wanted to know for himself which laws were good for the American people and which laws were holding them back.

The Constitution
After the United States became a country, a list of laws was created for it to follow. The Constitution could be adapted, with amendments, but at this time, it still allowed slavery.

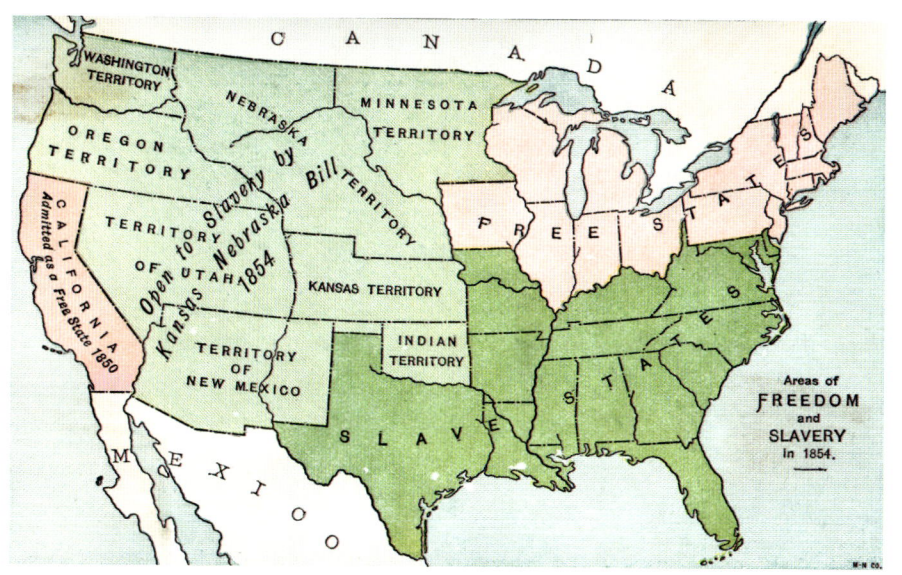

Lincoln spoke out against slavery. At that time, slavery was allowed by the Constitution. Half of the states in the country no longer permitted slavery, but the other half did. When the country took over new land, people argued over whether these new territories should be free or adopt slavery.

Lincoln thought they should be free. In his mind, slavery was a disease, and it must not be allowed to spread any farther.

Building a Family

When Lincoln met Mary Todd, she seemed like his opposite. Though he was popular, he was tall, awkward, and poor. Some people made fun of the ungraceful way he walked. Mary was short, charming, and rich. She spoke French, wore fancy dresses, and knew all the latest dance steps.

The Lincoln home in Springfield, Illinois

Mary Todd   Tad and Lincoln

1864 political cartoon of Lincoln

But Abe and Mary had much in common. Both had lost their mothers at a young age. They both loved poetry. Both were strong-minded but also open to new ideas. Mary had been raised by a father who enslaved people, yet she came to believe that slavery was wrong.

Abe and Mary married in 1842. Within a year, they had a son, Robert. Their second son, Edward, died when he was three. Next came Willie, then Thomas, who went by the nickname Tad. Abe doted on his boys, especially little Tad.

From Congress to Countryside

In 1847, Lincoln was elected to the US Congress. Moving to the nation's capital was a big shock. Washington, DC, was surrounded by two states that allowed slavery, Maryland and Virginia. Slavery was legal in the city, too. Even President James K. Polk enslaved Black people, four of whom worked and lived in the White House. Lincoln proposed a law to end slavery in the city.

Enslaved people were bought and sold in the nation's capital.

US Congress
Congress is the lawmaking branch of the government. It has two parts: the House of Representatives and the Senate. Each state sends two senators to the Senate. The number of representatives a state has depends on its population.

At that time, all the land from Texas to California was part of Mexico. Mexico had abolished slavery. But Polk planned to steal that land and bring slavery back into it. Lincoln also argued against the war Polk started there.

Lincoln's ideas were dismissed. When he ran for reelection, he lost. But still, his strong arguments had impressed everyone, even those who disagreed with him.

Back in Illinois, Lincoln became one of those traveling lawyers he had admired as a boy. He rode all over the state, setting up court wherever there was a dispute. Abe looked for the facts in each argument. Then, he presented his solution. Sometimes, it was like being a detective, and sometimes like being a salesman.

This job was good practice for the job he really wanted—US senator. Lincoln believed the whole country needed new laws to fit the problems of the day.

But to get the job, Lincoln would have to defeat the very popular Stephen Douglas. Douglas was a great public speaker, and Lincoln even agreed with most of his policies. They disagreed on one big issue: slavery. Neither man thought slavery was right for America. But Lincoln also thought it was evil. And he was determined to make voters see it that way, too.

The Eighth Circuit Court served all of Illinois. The judge, Lincoln, and other lawyers traveled on horseback, then on newly built railroads.

Candidate Once More

Huge crowds gathered to hear Lincoln and Douglas debate. Lincoln demanded to know what gave one person the right to own another. Douglas argued that Black people were not truly people, equal to whites. Douglas asked: What rights did Lincoln plan on giving them? Should they vote? Become senators? Go back to Africa?

Lincoln wasn't sure. He hadn't known very many Black people. And he lived in a time when very few white people wanted equality for all Americans.

US or Africa?
Before the Civil War, many white people thought the best thing for enslaved Black people would be for the government to buy their freedom and send them to Africa. Lincoln agreed with this plan at first. But men like activist Frederick Douglass convinced him this was not what most Black people born in America wanted.

Election poster showing Abe with his running mate, Hannibal Hamlin.

Douglas was reelected. But Lincoln had been brilliant in the debates, and the whole country was paying attention. He became so popular that he decided to skip the Senate. He would run for president.

He promised to do everything in his power to stop the spread of slavery. "If slavery is not wrong," he said, "then nothing is wrong."

Still, Lincoln didn't want to cause trouble. He saw the United States as a big family, with each state as a member. He admitted that the country was currently "a house divided" over the issue of slavery. But he had faith that eventually things would work out.

Abolitionist Sojourner Truth had escaped from slavery at age 30.

For the first time, a presidential candidate was saying that slavery was wrong. Lincoln was not planning on abolishing slavery, but enslavers were afraid of what he might do once he gained power.

Abolitionists

Some people wanted to abolish slavery immediately, no matter what the Constitution said about it. They were called abolitionists. Lincoln was willing to wait for slavery to end gradually. But the Civil War would change his mind.

Lincoln talking with Union officers in Maryland, October 3, 1862

Wartime President

In 1860, Lincoln was elected president, but just barely. No southern state wanted him. By the time the Lincolns moved into the White House, the country had fallen apart.

South Carolina quit the country first, followed by Mississippi, Florida, Alabama, Georgia, Louisiana, Texas, Virginia, Arkansas, North Carolina, and Tennessee. They called themselves the Confederate States of America, or the Confederacy.

Jefferson Davis

They elected their own president, Jefferson Davis. They made a new flag. They wrote a constitution that would protect slavery forever.

Lincoln didn't know what to do. The US Constitution didn't say whether states could break away from the US, also called the Union. Lincoln asked his advisers, all of whom had more political experience than he did. But no one could agree on a plan.

One thing was certain, however. The Confederacy had a powerful army, and it was just across the river from the White House.

Secession
States had threatened to leave, or secede from, the United States before the Civil War. But no states actually seceded until 1860.

The Confederates attacked first. They seized Fort Sumter, off the coast of Charleston, South Carolina.

Most people expected the conflict to last just a few weeks. Families brought picnic lunches to the first battlefield, expecting to watch the fighting. But this was real war, and within minutes, everyone was running for their lives. No one was prepared for what would be four years of death and destruction.

Fort Sumter under attack

Families were torn apart when sons fought on different sides. Farm boys who had never left their home states found themselves hundreds of miles away, shooting at other farm boys.

Lincoln visited the Union troops, trying to offer some comfort. As president, he was leader of the US military. Each decision was ultimately his responsibility. He slept very little. He aged very fast.

Lincoln, 1858

Lincoln, 1865

Robert (below), Willie (right)

Willie and Tad with Lincoln cousin Lockwood Todd

In 1862, Lincoln's 11-year-old son Willie came down with a fever. The doctors had no idea what was wrong. Little Tad got sick, too, but he got better. Willie did not.

This was the second boy the Lincolns had lost. And now Robert, their oldest son, wanted to join the Union army. Mary wouldn't hear of it. Abe didn't want to risk Robert's life either, but millions of parents were losing sons in the war. Keeping his own boy safe wouldn't be fair.

Later that year, one of the bloodiest battles of the war was fought just 70 miles from the White House. At Antietam, Maryland, thousands of soldiers died, and more than 17,000 were wounded. The Union won the battle, but no one felt like celebrating.

An Unexpected Friendship

Lincoln had never wanted war. But he was determined something good must come from it.

Frederick Douglass was a well-respected abolitionist. He encouraged Lincoln. Douglass urged Lincoln to use the war to rid the country of slavery forever. The two men became friends. Abe came to realize that they truly were equals. Yet the color of Douglass's skin prevented him from being an American citizen. He wasn't even allowed to vote.

Frederick Douglass
Born into slavery, Douglass secretly taught himself to read. At the age of 20, he escaped. He dedicated his life to the abolition of slavery and to civil rights. He was a powerful writer and public speaker. He challenged racist laws and attitudes.

Lincoln's own mind had not been as open as he'd thought. Douglass asked why Black men weren't allowed to be soldiers in the army, to fight for their own freedom. Lincoln couldn't answer. After all, Black soldiers had fought in the Revolutionary War.

In 1863, the first Black regiment of the Civil War was formed. The army insisted they be led by a white man, but at least they could fight against the system that had oppressed Black people for hundreds of years.

The War on Slavery

Lincoln hated war, but he was determined not to let all those soldiers die for no reason. He fired his top general for being too timid. He demanded that men who hadn't yet joined the fight must volunteer.

Many thought Lincoln was going too far, acting more like a king than a president—especially when he shocked the world with his Emancipation Proclamation. From that moment on, it said, enslaved people in the Confederacy were free. However, Lincoln didn't outlaw slavery in states that hadn't joined the Confederacy, such as Maryland. He wanted to keep the loyal states happy.

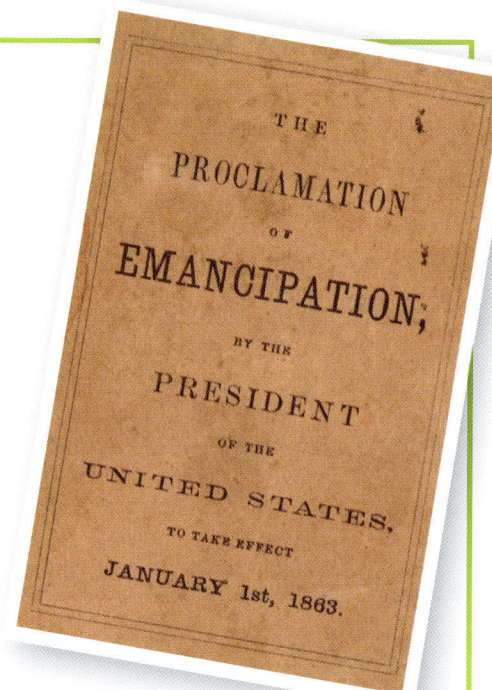

Abolitionists hated how limited the proclamation was. Confederate states ignored it. Lincoln wasn't *their* president, after all.

Still, Lincoln had given the war meaning. Most wars are fought to get more power or land. This war was against slavery.

In 1863, the Fourth of July was not a day for celebration. In the battle at Gettysburg, Pennsylvania, more than 50,000 soldiers had been killed, wounded, or captured, or had gone missing. Lincoln later visited the battlefield, where a cemetery had been built. He offered a few words to honor the dead. He tried to make sense of what they'd died for.

Hard to Hear
At Gettysburg, speeches were given outdoors to a huge crowd. Lincoln's voice was thin and shrill, so most people who were there probably didn't catch any of his extremely short speech.

Lincoln delivering the Gettysburg Address

Not many people could hear him. Those who could were not impressed. The speech only lasted a couple of minutes. But what is now known as the Gettysburg Address became one of the most famous speeches of all time.

Lincoln reminded Americans that their country had begun with a war, fought to gain freedom. He said they must work to make sure the country was truly free for all its people. It was every citizen's responsibility to make sure "that government of the people, by the people, for the people" would never be allowed to end.

Lincoln's second inauguration, March 4, 1865

The Last Casualty of the War

In 1864, Lincoln's first term as president was coming to an end. Many people thought the election should be canceled because of the war. But Lincoln didn't think a country without free elections would be worth fighting for.

His opponent was George McClellan, the general he had fired. McClellan promised peace, even if it meant slavery would continue. So many people wanted the war to end that Lincoln didn't expect to win the election.

George McClellan

On election night, it wasn't clear that Lincoln would win. But then more votes came in from the army and navy. The soldiers believed in Lincoln's mission.

Lincoln won the election. He would have four more years to lead the country back to peace, and forward to freedom. Lincoln had always respected the US Constitution, but he realized it needed fixing. He asked Congress to amend or add to it. The 13th Amendment would make slavery illegal all across the country.

On April 9, 1865, the Confederacy surrendered. The states were united once again. But what about the people? How would millions of newly freed Americans live alongside the same people who had oppressed them?

Abe would never know. Just a few days after the war ended, the Lincolns went to Ford's Theatre to enjoy a comedy. A famous actor named John Wilkes Booth was there waiting for Lincoln, with a gun. Booth thought killing Lincoln might still save the Confederacy. He snuck up behind the president and shot him in the head. Lincoln died the next morning.

John Wilkes Booth escaping after shooting Lincoln

Lincoln's funeral train

Lincoln's body was taken back to Illinois on a funeral train. It stopped in eleven cities to let people say goodbye.

When historians rank US presidents, Lincoln nearly always tops the list. He spent his lifetime trying to learn and improve himself. He surrounded himself with advisers who would challenge him. His views of slavery and equality evolved over time. Perhaps it was his open mind that made him such a great leader.

Glossary

Abolitionist
A person who worked to make slavery illegal

Amendment
An addition to a document that changes it in some way

Candidate
A person who is running for an elected office

Civil War
A war fought in the United States from 1861 to 1865, between Americans in northern states and Americans in southern states, primarily over the issue of slavery

Confederate
Belonging to the Confederacy, a country made of states that wanted to separate from the United States

Constitution
A document that gives the basic laws and principles of a nation and describes the rights of its citizens

Debate
To talk publicly about different ideas, often as part of a political election

Dispute
An argument or disagreement

Emancipation Proclamation
A document issued by Abraham Lincoln that freed enslaved people in the Confederacy

Enslaved
Living in slavery, forced to work without pay

Legislature
The part of a government that makes laws

Militia
A volunteer army

Oppress
To crush by abuse of power

Population
The number of people living in a place

Senator
A person elected to represent a region or state in the government

Slavery
The practice of owning people and forcing them to work without pay

Union
The states that remained part of the United States after 11 states seceded to form the Confederacy

Index

abolitionists 29, 36, 39
Antietam, Maryland 35
Black people 26, 36, 37
   see also slavery
Booth, John Wilkes 44
Bush, Sarah 10
Civil War
   battles 32–33, 35, 40
   Black soldiers 37
   Lincoln's
     responsibilities 4,
     33, 35, 38, 40–41
   slavery issue 29, 36,
     39, 41, 43–44
   surrender of
     Confederacy 44
Confederacy 30–32,
   39, 44
Constitution, US 18, 19,
   29, 31, 43
Davis, Jefferson 31
Douglas, Stephen 24,
   26, 27, 28
Douglass, Frederick
   26, 36–37
Emancipation
   Proclamation 39
enslaved people see
   slavery
Ford's Theatre 44
Fort Sumter 32
Franklin, Benjamin 10,
   11
Gettysburg Address
   40–41
Hamlin, Hannibal 28
Illinois legislature
   16–18

lawyers 12, 13, 18, 24,
   25
Lincoln, Abraham
   childhood 6–11
   death 44–45
   as great leader 45
   Illinois legislature
     17–18
   as lawyer 18, 24, 25
   marriage 21
   in militia 16
   presidency 4, 30–31,
     33, 35–43
   presidential
     reelection 42–43
   school and learning
     8, 10–11, 15
   slavery beliefs 7, 14,
     19, 24, 26, 28–29
   US Congress 22, 23
   US Senate campaign
     24, 26–28
Lincoln, Edward 21
Lincoln, Mary Todd
   20–21, 35
Lincoln, Robert 21, 34,
   35
Lincoln, Sarah Bush 10
Lincoln, Sarah (sister)
   8
Lincoln, Thomas "Tad"
   21, 34, 35
Lincoln, Willie 21, 34,
   35
McClellan, George 43
militia 16
Mississippi River 14
Native Americans 7, 16

New Orleans 14
Polk, James K. 22–23
presidency 4, 30–31,
   33, 35–43
secession 30, 31
slavery
   abolitionists 29, 36,
     39
   back to Africa plan
     26
   Confederacy 31, 39
   Douglas's beliefs 24,
     26
   Emancipation
     Proclamation 39
   Lincoln's beliefs 7,
     14, 19, 24, 26,
     28–29
   Mary Todd Lincoln's
     beliefs 21
   slave markets 14
   US Constitution 18,
     43
   where it was legal 7,
     19, 22–23, 39
Todd, Lockwood 34
Todd, Mary 20–21, 35
traveling courts 12, 13,
   24, 25
Truth, Sojourner 29
Union troops 33, 35
US Congress 22, 23
US Constitution 18, 19,
   29, 31, 43
US Senate campaign
   24, 26–28
Washington, George
   10, 11
White House 22

47

Quiz

Answer the questions to see what you have learned. Check your answers in the key below.

1. In which state was Abraham Lincoln born?
2. What year was Lincoln first elected president?
3. What was the name of the document that was written to free enslaved people in the Confederacy?
4. Which amendment to the Constitution made slavery illegal?
5. True or False: Most of the people at Gettysburg could hear every word of Lincoln's Gettysburg Address.

1. Kentucky 2. 1860 3. The Emancipation Proclamation
4. The 13th Amendment 5. False